FINDING
PEACE

Jean Vanier

FINDING
PEACE

ANANSI

Published in 2003 by
House of Anansi Press Inc.
110 Spadina Ave., Suite 801
Toronto, ON, M5V 2K4
Tel. 416-363-4343
Fax 416-363-1017
www.anansi.ca

Distributed in Canada by
Publishers Group Canada
250A Carlton Street
Toronto, ON, M5A 2L1
Tel. 416-934-9900
Toll free order numbers:
Tel. 800-663-5714
Fax 800-565-3770

07 06 05 04 03   1 2 3 4 5

National Library of Canada Cataloguing in Publication

Vanier, Jean, 1928–
Finding peace / Jean Vanier.

ISBN 0-88784-683-1

1. Peace of mind. 2. Peace. 3. Spiritual life. I. Title.

B105.P4V35 2003   248.4'82   C2002-905752-3

Cover and book design: Bill Douglas
Typesetting: Brian Panhuyzen

Printed and bound in Canada

Canada Council   Conseil des Arts
for the Arts   du Canada

*We acknowledge for their financial support of our publishing program the Canada
Council for the Arts, the Ontario Arts Council, and the Government of Canada
through the Book Publishing Industry Development Program (BPIDP).*

Contents

INTRODUCTION

THE EVENTS OF September 11, 2001, shocked the American people and the whole world. They occurred shortly after President Bush announced the creation of a blanket, a shield over the United States that would prevent enemy missiles from targeting the country. The destruction of the twin towers and the attack on the Pentagon, however, were executed from inside the country, by men who had been trained as pilots on American soil.

The shock of the attacks generated anger in the hearts of many Westerners towards Arabs and Muslims, people whose cultures were so unfamiliar and seemingly different from our own. New walls of racism, prejudice, and fear arose, and the West began to prepare for a long war against terrorism. People compared September 11 to Pearl Harbor and called for swift retaliation. The president quickly allocated billions of dollars more to the military, sent troops to Afghanistan, and launched a battle against terrorism.

For weeks after September 11, people everywhere lived in fear. Would there be another attack? When? Where would it come from? Would there be chemical warfare?

When I was told about the attacks and was invited to see the pictures on television, I refused. I felt far too fragile and vulnerable to look at the destruction and to watch people leaping to their death from the top floors of the towers. I knew that these images would remain in my imagination and have a power over me, holding me in fear and inner turmoil. It wasn't that I wanted to run away from reality, but that I needed to keep my heart in sufficient peace to pray and to be present to reality and to people and situations around me. The events of September 11 called me to become personally committed to peacemaking, to continue to reflect on peace and on the sources of violence in our world, in me, and in each one of us.

People from various cultures and religions, as well as people with no specific religious tradition came together after the attacks to pray and to affirm together their vision of mutual acceptance and their esteem and love for all human beings. And yet the evenings of prayer I participated in left me a bit uneasy. I felt as though people were not praying for a new just order between people and nations, but, motivated by fear, were praying to keep the status quo — no change, no insecurity, nothing that would disturb their lives or views on the world.

But a few people started asking pertinent questions: Why don't Arab or Islamic countries like us? Why don't poorer countries like us? Haven't we given them money and helped them to become more democratic? What is behind these attacks? The questions they were asking weren't so much how to respond to such vicious assaults, which obviously no government could leave unpunished, but how to understand where the hate was coming from and how to respond to that hate, how to break down the barriers that separate people and cultures.

One of the deepest human desires and needs is to live in peace, to be in peace — but hatred, fear, and violence seem so prevalent, and sometimes our world seems to have lost its bearings and become mad with suicide bombings, hostage takings, and war mongering. We don't appear to know where we are going or what we want. We all yearn for peace, but what is it exactly? Is it just the absence of war? How can we find peace? What are the origins of conflict? How should we act when faced with conflict? How can we resolve conflict? How do we become peacemakers?

My hope is that more and more people will discover that the peace we all yearn for is not just the
work of governments but the task of each one of us.
We can all become makers of peace. We can do our
part. The future of the world is in the hands of each of
us, and it depends on our commitment together with
others for peace, each according to our own gifts and
responsibilities. Peace is not a question just of stopping this or that catastrophe, but of rediscovering a
vision, a path of hope for all of humanity.

The past thirty-eight years living at L'Arche with
men and women with intellectual disabilities have
formed and nourished me for these reflections on
peace and conflict. In some ways my whole adult life
has been oriented towards peacemaking. In 1942, in
the middle of the Second World War, I joined the
Royal Naval College in England because I wanted to
be part of the struggle for peace and freedom. I left
the navy in 1950 because I felt called to work in
another way for peace and freedom, to better understand the causes of conflict and the way to resolve
them through a deepening in spirituality and in a
love that flows from the heart of God. The founding
of L'Arche in 1964 was part of that journey: its mission is to give a home to the homeless and respect to
those who have been rejected. I wanted to share my

life with those who were weak, and with them to create communities of peace. At the beginning there was a lot of violence in our communities as many of our residents came from oppressive situations and were filled with a lot of anger and anguish. So dealing with violence was part of our everyday life. And so these reflections do not come from any experience in negotiating peace between countries or ethnic groups — I do not have any political background as such — but from my immediate experience of people and their growth in trust and in peace.

Etty Hillesum, a Dutch Jewish woman killed in the gas chambers of Auschwitz, wrote, "After this war two torrents will be unleashed on the world: a torrent of loving kindness and a torrent of hatred. I knew that I should struggle against hatred."[1] I would like to make those words mine. I would like them to echo through me. In her diary Etty wrote about her reflections on life, her spiritual growth, and her understanding of humanity. She, who had no formal religious education as such, wrote about her experience of God. I think she is one of the great prophets of peace of our time, able to enlighten those who are anxious about the state of our world today. Her wisdom and love were born and grew as she and her fellow Jews lived some of their darkest hours. They were oppressed, crushed, hunted out, targeted for elimination. This planned genocide of a whole race remains one of the bleakest moments in the history of humanity. Yet, through it all, Etty opened up a road of hope and peace.

And I believe we can learn to do the same. As we live through the fear and conflict that resulted from September 11, we should not despair. We *can* find the road to hope and peace in our world if we open ourselves to change, enter into true relationships, and break down the walls around own hearts. I believe that even today we can unleash a torrent of loving kindness that will bring peace to our world.

I

CONFLICT AND FEAR

IN AN EASTERN EUROPEAN village I once visited, half the villagers were Roman Catholic and the other half Orthodox. I asked about ecumenism and was told that the two halves never interacted with each other. Each had their own churches and schools; they even bought things only from people of their own church. They never met.

This small village, for all intents and purposes, lived in peace. There was no violence, no conflict, no breach of any laws. And yet within it lay the same tension that sparks so much conflict within our *global* village: isolation, separation, and apparent indifference to one another. It is human nature to protect what is precious to us behind defensive walls. We erect borders and boundaries to protect our nations, our cultures, our families, our certitudes and our own hearts. We are only too familiar with the conflicts in Kashmir, the Middle East, Northern Ireland, the Russian Federation, and many other places, over political boundaries. But we rarely take the time to look closely at the barricades we erect in our daily lives, as we interact with neighbours and family. And we confront even less frequently the personal fears that prevent us from reaching out in fellowship to others to build the road to peace and hope.

Cultural Conflict

People are born into a culture and a religion that inform their attitudes and ways of life. Each tradition has its own language, ways of dressing, rituals around food and worship, and ways of celebrating marriage, birth, and death. Culture forms our identity. We know who we are because we know our ancestry, culture, race, and religion.

Cultural and national groups are strong and coherent. Each has its own certitudes; each group seems to know that it is "right," "chosen," "blessed by God" or by the gods. And to affirm its identity it seeks to defend itself from other groups or so often to dominate them, to show how wonderful, right and powerful it is, and to gain land for its expanding population. For such a group to have God's blessing means to have power, and to have power is to become like God the Almighty, omnipotent and above us all. Power is a sign of greatness, but when it is exercised to distinguish between the work of God accomplished by so-called good people of our group and the work of so-called evildoers, it can quickly justify the grave injustices we know today — in Afghanistan, in Kosovo, in Northern Ireland, and elsewhere.

The causes of conflicts and wars are multiple, but often they find their origin in difference and in the forging of identity through culture and religion. The bond among people of the same culture or ethnic group gives them security, a firm sense of solidarity, and a kind of peace — albeit a limited peace, reserved for those in their group (or at least for those who can and do follow the laws of the group — so often people with disabilities can be excluded from the group). Conflicts arise when groups or individuals need to show that their way is right, that they have power, and want to dominate and lord over others. The Crusades and wars of religion were almost always waged with hatred and cruelty "in the name of God." And in more recent times, one has only to think of Nazi Germany and the Holocaust, or of Stalin crushing the Christian church and killing so many people in the Soviet Union. Throughout the history of humanity we see the need to create an empire based on the power of one group and the elimination of others.

Political Conflict

The history of colonization is revealing and sad. Powerful, rich European countries went to Africa, the Americas, the Pacific, and Asia to conquer and obtain new natural resources. They destroyed local cultures, some in which there was no gap between rich and poor and where collective power was used in a positive way to defend, nourish, and protect the members of the tribe or group. In many instances the colonizers gave limited power and education to a select few they had conquered, who in turn quickly used this new power, wealth, and education to dominate those in their own country who were poorer and weaker. To those who have it, power can bring a sense of freedom and an opportunity to gain more wealth and prestige. But it can also enslave in despair and lack of opportunity those who are disenfranchised, making them less human, victims of the powerful. The powerful oppose change; they want to maintain and develop their own riches and power. If the powerless start rising up, expressing their needs, seeking power, land, better jobs and pay for themselves, then those in power will lose some of their wealth and privileges. As Majed Nassar and Nassar Ibrahim note in their book *Cry Freedom*, "in any colonial relationship, the colonialists know what is good for themselves as well as for the colonized, who are too 'primitive' to understand what is in their own interest. Those who are colonized are voiceless, by definition. When they attempt to express themselves, they are always considered to be overly emotional and irrational."[2] Ironically, history shows that often oppressed people spend most of their energy struggling against their oppressors, and when they eventually do attain power, they themselves begin to oppress others. They do not learn to use their energies to create community, develop their own culture, and deepen their sense of identity, as Nelson Mandela sought to do for South Africa.

History books from different countries and cultures tell different stories, depending on who is perceived as "good" and who as "bad." One has only to read the story of the Crusades as written by the Arabs, the Greeks, and the French to see how difficult it is to grasp the truth. Read about the birth of modern Israel from the Zionist perspective and then from the Palestinian point of view, and you have totally different stories.

For the Romans at the time of Jesus it was evident that only military strength could solve political problems, enforce "peace," and prevent small countries from fighting each other. But can peace today flow from a military power that is feared and imposed on people? Our armies carry out so-called peace missions, but they do not necessarily make peace, just stop the fighting. United Nations troops have been in Cyprus for forty years, enforcing the ceasefire between Greek and Turkish islanders — but this is not peace. This is the status quo, an enforced separation and isolation of two cultures. True peace can rarely be imposed from the outside; it must be born within and between communities through meetings and dialogue and then carried outward.

Societal Conflict

The world is divided into many thousands of more or less hermetically closed groups. If each group is sure that it is better than others, how can peace ever come? It is difficult to dialogue with others if we cling arrogantly to the idea that we are right or that our power and technology are a sign of our humanity and goodness. Walls and barriers exist between people because of language, but also because of fear — each group fearful of those who are different, fearful of losing its identity. People resist opening up to others. Aren't we all in one way or another enclosed in a secure group, in our culture, our religion, our family, our network of friends? Family and different types of groups are needed for human growth, but when they become sealed they engender rivalry, conflict, elitism.

Soon after the founding of L'Arche, a woman came to see me. She had some old clothes and worn-out shoes that she wanted to give to the men we had welcomed. Her intention was surely kind, but I felt her vision was patronizingly distorted — as if she were offering garbage to people who are garbage. Why do we want to give away things that we ourselves do not value? Is it to have a good conscience? Is it just the *need* to give? It would be more helpful and important for someone like this woman to have a personal encounter with people with disabilities, to see their value, their gifts, and their capacity to express their own needs.

Many rich and powerful groups want to help those who are poor and weak. This can be very worthy, but frequently they regard the others as inferior, incapable of helping themselves, meriting only condescension and pity. These people may be generous and want to "do good" for others, but they want to give according to *their* terms and policies, from their positions of superiority and power. They are unable to listen to people from another social sphere or culture, and so are unable to appreciate that culture. They do not help people to express themselves and to grow in self-esteem; they do not reveal to them their value. People in authority tend to control situations, as they are frightened of change or of what might happen if those of another social sphere are free to become themselves.

In many cosmopolitan societies such as Canada and the United States, people of different cultures, backgrounds, and religions can and do live "peacefully" side by side. There is often mutual respect, civility, and acceptance of laws that protect the rights of each person and each minority group. There is no civil war. This respect for each other and for the law can, nevertheless, harbour certain prejudices and forms of racism. People can, and often do, avoid one another. Immigrants are allowed to live in certain areas but not in others. People with disabilities can be looked down upon. Subtle forms of anti-Semitism or anti-Arabism are practised. Even though there is a certain respect for difference among neighbours, there is rarely any desire to enter into personal relationships. People close themselves off, ignoring and avoiding others.

Can peace be simply this politeness, civility, and respect for law? These elements are, of course, the beginning of peace, but the walls that protect people and cultures still hold firm. In some countries this civil or polite acceptance of others, this coexistence, can quickly be disturbed by rumours, propaganda, or events that create fear and mutual suspicion. For example, one can easily imagine that if Quebec separated from the rest of Canada enmity and violence could arise between Canadians and Quebecers. In

Rwanda, Tutsis and Hutus coexisted side by side in the same villages for many years, but, little by little, through false rumours and subtle propaganda, they became estranged from each other. Many Hutus came to believe that their Tutsi neighbours were planning to kill them, so the Hutus struck first. Hutus and Tutsis together suffered a continual distortion of the truth: propaganda and lies provoked doubt and suspicion, which broke down trust and engendered fear. Fear led to hatred, hatred led to conflict, and atrocities and terror were born.

FAMILY CONFLICT

We often experience conflict most directly within our own homes, in the arguments and hurts that can accompany family life and growing up. Parents, however loving and wonderful they may be, sometimes have difficulty accepting their children as they are and may treat a child unjustly, provoking deep, non-verbalized anger. This anger can fester and awaken many forms of violence. Parents may be more open and loving to one child than to others, creating jealousy and rivalry. An elder brother may bully a younger one. Children can have multiple conflicting feelings: the desire to be loved and the fear of not being loveable, the fear of being beaten or abandoned. Such feelings awaken anguish, which is a source of depression and of violence. Conflicts or the refusal to communicate between husband and wife can also engender fear and insecurity in their children. Since children are often powerless to respond to their parents and cannot flourish in insecurity, a hidden violence is generated in them that manifests itself later in life in multiple forms. Fear of ourselves, a broken self-image, lack of self-esteem, and violence can be implanted in us all at an early age and to varying degrees.

Parents need to educate their children and lead them as far as they can to the truth of human existence. The most fundamental role for a parent is to help children believe in themselves, in their own value, and to develop their personal conscience, not just to fit into society according to parental desires or the pressures of their peer group.

CONFLICT WITHIN OURSELVES

What is true for cultures, countries, and families is also true for individuals. Don't we all want to prove that we are right and others wrong? Don't we want to show how strong and good we are? Don't we need to prove that we have value? Don't we need to feel that we are successful and held in esteem by others, that we excel in some way?

Competition and rivalry seem to be the basis of

many things in our culture. We all need to be successful, winners. Competition is, of course, important and
valuable. It calls forth new energies that help people
move forward, be creative, and grow in competence in
their own domain. But if competition can have value,
we also see the inherent danger in a society *based* on
competition. In such a society there are few winners,
many losers, and even more victims. Some people
gravitate to the top; others drop into the pits of depression, jealousy, and anger — anger with themselves,
their parents, society, the church, God, everyone who
seems to have cheated them out of happiness.

When we are made to feel inferior through a lack
of respect for our deepest needs, we often begin to
accept the vision of the powerful and to believe that
we *are* inferior, that we should just do what we are
told. We submit to those who have power, lose our
self-esteem, and enter into a form of depression. We
might also want to become like those who have
power, copying their values and aggressive attitudes
and developing a sense of ourselves that is based on
oppression of the weak — or maybe we will close up
in anger and revolt against those who have power.
Either way, we can lose faith in ourselves. Rather than
developing and deepening our own vision of life, we
use up our energies in obeying or attacking others
and their system of values. When we lose ourselves,

it is much easier to latch onto what is outside than what is inside — easier to identify ourselves against an other than to search within our deepest needs and yearnings.

Fear incites us to hide behind the walls of our heart, our group, our community. It is so deep within us all. We want security, but often that means forgetting who we are in our deepest self. We are frightened of *not being*: not being loved, not being a success, not being appreciated or seen as worthy, not having a place if we leave the security of our group. We can be frightened of loneliness and anguish. Consumed by this fear, we seek out those who we think are preventing us from becoming what we want to be, those who are "out to get us." They are the rivals, seeking what we want. Strangely, we can even harbour a fear of peace, because we think we might lose something if there is peace. So we continue the fighting and the rivalry.

We human beings are not God. We are not the saviours of the world. We do not have all life within us. There will always be an emptiness in us, a deep vulnerability, an anguish, an unfulfilled thirst, a place of dissatisfaction. We are constantly yearning to move out of the prison of the limited, searching for what we hope will totally fulfill us. We are always looking for more. And once we have attained the treasure, we quickly become dissatisfied again, like a child who wants another toy, more toys! If we don't have this *more* we tend to find fault in another person who does have more, who is stopping us from getting more. We judge and condemn the "other," the one who is different and has something we do not have. We are profoundly jealous because we do not have the fullness of life in us. We are frightened of recognizing our own brokenness or faults or weakness, just as we can be frightened of recognizing what is deepest within us, our inner beauty and value.

Despite all our barriers, all the rubble that blocks the path to peace of heart, I gain hope in the many examples of people who strive and nourish freedom within individual hearts. I think of the wonderful work over the past twenty years of Jacqueline, a woman who lives near Bethlehem and works with Palestinian children from all over the West Bank, teaching them songs and dances and thereby helping them discover and maintain their dignity, giving them a voice, a way to express and share a human freedom that cannot be suppressed.

FINDING FREEDOM

If we are fearful of *not being* and of those who might push us into the pit of not being, is it not because we are frightened of death?

Death is the final passage to our ultimate resting place, where the yearning for the infinite in us will rest and rejoice in the Infinite, where we will never cease to grow and be amazed in the discovery of the Infinite. I remember hearing the story of a white torturer in South Africa telling Nelson Mandela, "Don't you know that I have the power to have you killed?" Mandela answered, "Don't you know that I have the power to go to my death freely?" We find freedom as we accept and believe in ourselves, mortal as we are, not pretending to be anything else. A friend of mine lived for a few weeks in a hospital where many patients were undergoing radiation therapy. Some of them were in acute pain and anxiety. What struck my friend was that conversations between the patients always seemed to be centred on God and faith. When one is in pain or weakness or close to death, one begins to share ideas about what is essential, one's deepest concerns and hopes. No one is a threat to anyone. On the contrary, people begin to open their hearts to one another.

In our technologically developed societies, death can be seen as an accident, something that should *not be*, a surprise caused by another or by an unseen hand. We fear and resist death, imagining it as an "other," as something unnatural and outside ourselves. And yet it is inscribed in our genes. Freud wrote in his essay on death that the person who wants to live fully must prepare for death. "Look death in the face. . . . Don't run away from it; don't pretend it doesn't exist."³

I am touched by the vision of palliative care that was created by Lady Cecily Saunders. My sister Thérèse worked with her for many years in St. Christopher's Hospice in London, caring for people who were dying, particularly cancer patients, in order to help them leave this life humanely, peacefully, fully conscious, and with no pain. With good help during their times of anguish and despair, many are able to say just before their death, "I am ready now." It is a pity that we have to wait until our last breath to accept who we are! Let us not be afraid of ourselves and of our being. Let us not submit grudgingly to our lives and all that happens. Let us choose life in truth and freedom, which also means accepting and welcoming death when it comes. If we do, we begin to accept the many little deaths of life — disappointments, failures, rejections, different forms of hurt — and to penetrate the walls of our own complacency and recognize the need for change.

II

THE NEED FOR CHANGE

Let me begin by telling a parable that may seem funny, but in fact is not funny at all. It is only too true!

A factory supervisor yells at one of his workers, who cannot answer back without losing his job; the worker returns home and vents his anger and anguish on his wife, who has not prepared the meal on time. She doesn't dare answer back, but vents her anger and anguish on her son when she sees him taking something from the refrigerator. Her son doesn't answer back, but vents his anger on the dog, which runs after the cat, which eats up a mouse! So often we seek to hurt others because we ourselves have been hurt.

When one has been put down unjustly or bullied by someone who is stronger, one tends to want revenge, but also to turn one's anger upon someone who is weaker. When parents are hard on their children, those children risk being hard on their own children later on. We tend to give what we have received. We are frightened of standing up to a stronger person. So it is that those who are the weakest and have no voice are pushed aside. This is particularly true for women who for a long time were not fully recognized as people or who have been abused sexually, for children who are abused, and for people with disabilities who cannot defend themselves. Peace can come only if the chain of violence and rejection is broken and the weaker members of society are fully welcomed, loved, and respected.

Conflict is a part of life because we are part of an evolving humanity. Each person, each group grows and changes. Life involves change. Some people resist change, and thus prevent growth; they want to maintain the status quo, to maintain their comfort, power, wealth, and certitudes. They do not and cannot accept loss. Others feel cheated, jealous, and angry because they have too little power, freedom, and comfort, and nobody really listens to them. They want to move ahead, to do more, to be more and have more. They revolt against those who have power. Adolescents, for example, can become angry with parents who don't accept them in their needs and desires, who give them everything except a love founded on respect. Conflict also arises in institutions such as churches that are in need of renewal, but face resistance from cultural traditionalists who say, "It has always been done like this." At the same time, the too-new can often be too far removed from the vision and the tradition that give life.

We can understand that insolent might and dictatorial powers create a world of oppression, genocide, injustice, and we can understand that we must stand up to such inhuman power. But how awful it is to know that benevolent power too can hurt people and prevent them from finding inner liberation, from growing to a greater consciousness, from developing according to their deepest self. We can too easily live and perpetuate a travesty of love — doing "good things," as the woman who wanted to give us her old clothes, in order to make people what we want them to be or to be admired for our goodness. Is it possible to truly love people as they are, for themselves and for their inner freedom?

The universality of conflict is terribly depressing. We can be so frightened of conflict that we don't dare look at it or search for its cause in order to confront it. We pretend that everything will be all right or that we cannot do anything about it, and so we hide from reality and remain closed up in our own little world of illusion. Peace is not so much about suppressing conflict as it is about working through it, in a dialogue where each group or person feels respected, not put down or treated as someone inferior, someone who cannot understand. It *is* possible to mend what is broken. It is possible to bring peace and unity where there is conflict and division. But for that we need to be constantly transformed through humility; we need "a higher power," a new inner strength, a deeper wisdom and freedom, a new understanding of our evolving humanity and the reasons for necessary conflict.

In the 1970s I was asked to meet a man imprisoned in Montreal for killing five women. He was like a block of ice; vibrations of hate seemed to flow from him. I cannot remember if we talked or not, I just remember the terrible feeling of unease I experienced as I stood in his presence. Yet I could almost read his history. Around his heart he must have built up layers and layers of barriers to protect himself. He had probably been unwanted, physically or sexually abused as a child. If he had always been treated as a *thing* to be used or controlled and never as a person, how could he trust anyone? How could he trust himself? How could he change?

Many of us say, "If you change I will love you." But some people are discovering a different attitude about change and say, "You will change when you know that I love you — and then I too will change." A faithful commitment of love is necessary for people to open up and begin to change. At the basis of all human growth there must be self-esteem, a sense of one's deepest value as a person. We need to be seen as *persons*, not as things.

The book *Dead Man Walking* tells the story of Patrick Sonier, who, with his brother, murdered a young couple in a Louisiana park. Patrick was tried and condemned to death. Helen Prejean, a religious sister, was asked if she would befriend Patrick on death row. A friendship grew between them. Patrick discovered for the first time that he was loved, and so was loveable. Under all the layers of hate, violence, and despair, he discovered his true person, that he was unique and special. Helen revealed to him who he really was, his real value. Before he received the lethal injection, he looked at Helen, who was watching behind a glass pane, and said, "I love you." She looked at him and said, "I love you." Then he turned to the father of one of the people he had killed and said, "I am sorry." And he was executed.

Patrick found his true self because he was respected and loved, so he began to change. If people treat us only as evil, we remain evil. There can be peace only if we believe that people can change and can come out from behind their walls and barriers. "I no longer shut myself away in my room, God," wrote

Etty Hillesum. "I try to look things straight in the face, even the worst crimes, and to discover the small naked human being amidst the monstrous wreckage caused by man's senseless deeds."[4]

Some people see religion as the root cause of so much wreckage and conflict. My own feeling is that it is not so. At the heart of most, if not all, religions there is a call to become full of the compassion and goodness of God. We need to be grounded in our religion and culture, but also to see that the fulfillment of our culture and our religion is in universal love. In our place of faith and culture, in our church or religious tradition, we are called not only to love all that helps us be open to God and to others, but also to become aware of all that is not God in the way our faith is taught and lived — all that closes us up in ourselves, in our fears and prejudices. Religion can seal us off from others or open us up to them. I am called to listen to your way just as you are called to listen to mine. As we open our hearts to God and to one another, I discover how your way is leading you to truth, to compassion, and to God; you discover how my way is leading me to truth, to compassion, and to God. We gradually become like children, regaining some of our innocence and sincerity and contemplating the beauty of each other and our different ways to God and to peace.

I believe that at the core of many religions there is the desire, force, strength, and compassion to help all people to grow in freedom — to grow to be themselves. Recently the Pope brought leaders of all the world religions together at Assisi. They met and talked and prayed. Later they circulated a document, the "Assisi Decalogue of Peace," which embodied the spirit of their meeting: "We commit ourselves to educating people to mutual respect and esteem in order to bring about a peaceful and fraternal coexistence between people of different ethnic groups, cultures and religions." We see this force too in Mahatma Gandhi, whose great passion was to liberate the most oppressed of people and to help bring mutual respect to Hindus and Muslims. He understood that he could do nothing without God, "sole helper of the helpless."[5] The message of Jesus given in the gospel of John reveals that it *is* possible to do good for people, to love them, without possessing them or making them feel inferior. It *is* possible to bring people together in love.

I believe that anyone can change if he or she enters into a true relationship with someone. The man I met in Montreal was obviously a dangerous person who needed to be in prison. One day, perhaps, he will meet a prison chaplain, a visitor, a psychologist, someone like Helen Prejean, a guard, or another inmate who can awaken his deepest self and lead him to trust. But I am not naive. To love someone like this man, to enter into an authentic relationship with him and discover and reveal to him his true person, to trust in his capacity to change, requires tremendous skill, a lot of experience, a strong personality, and a deep love and fidelity over a long period of time.

When we no longer judge people, we discover that people of different cultures, like all of us, can change. All together we can become like a beautiful bouquet made up of many different flowers, or a wonderful symphony played by many instruments, each in harmony with the others. Isn't this the vision announced by the Jewish prophet Isaiah, when he foresaw a time when "the wolf shall dwell with the lamb and the leopard shall lie down with the kid and the calf and the lion shall feed together and a little child shall lead them"?[6]

There is a way to peace, a way of transcending cultures and crossing barriers, of going deeper into the world religions and into the heart of each person to discover the source of life, to discover that we are all called to have direct access to God, to listen to God and to universal truth, so that each of us — in our own way, wherever we are — becomes a man or woman of peace.

III

CROSSING THE BARRIERS AMONG US

DURING THE BALKAN WAR, a Serbian Orthodox priest hid and saved a number of Kosovites who were being sought by the Serbian army — he befriended "the enemy." However, when the Serbian army pulled out and the people of Kosovo sought revenge, this same priest hid and saved a number of Serbian civilians. Under similar circumstances, Captain Wilson Hosenfield of the German army, while stationed in Poland during the Second World War, saved the lives of many Jewish people at the risk of his own life. He hid and nourished Wladyslaw Szpilman, a Jewish pianist, who was being hunted by the SS.[7] The priest and the soldier were men of compassion, men of peace, entering into a true relationship with people who were different; seeing each person as a person, not just as a member of a group; redeeming the horrors caused by others. These men were no longer living under the shadow of category.

This passage, this crossing over the barricades that separate cultures and religions, is not a rejection of one's own faith, tradition, and culture, but rather a fulfillment of them. Faith, religion, and culture find their deepest meaning as they become a *way* to permit us to be bonded to God, the God of love and compassion, which give us the strength, the courage, and the wisdom to meet others who are different as *persons*. We can only be peacemakers if we believe that every person — whatever their culture, religion, values, abilities, or disabilities — is important and precious to God and if we seek to open our hearts to them.

Such encounters between people are deep, wonderful moments that seem to transcend time and space, religion and culture. They bring people together to a place of trust and mutual respect as they listen to one another and their sacred stories, not from the place of their own certitudes and ideologies, but from the place of inner silence. They imply a fundamental equality: no one person is superior to another. As we enter into this relationship together, we are opening our hearts to one another and somehow losing some of the things we want to possess in order to feel superior and to have power. Walls that separate culture, religion, social status, and people start to weaken in this gentle encounter.

RELATIONSHIP

Real peace implies something deeper than polite acceptance of those who are different. It means meeting those who are different, appreciating them and their culture, and creating bonds of friendship with them. Family, culture, religion, community, and friendship are all realities that are vital for human growth. But we need to learn how not to remain enclosed or imprisoned in such groups. We have to cross boundaries and meet others who are different. Coexistence is a foundation, and it is important, but peace is something much deeper. To create peace we have to go further than just saying hello. We have to discover who the other person is and reveal who we are. As we listen to and really meet one another, we begin to see the work of God in the beauty and value, in the deepest personhood, of those who are different.

In his book *I and Thou*, the Jewish philosopher Martin Buber speaks of relationship as the treasure of the human person; he distinguishes the "it" from the "thou." There are *things* and there are *people*, individual people. He reminds us that a society that encourages the accumulation of things — things to do, things to possess, things to look at, to buy, to throw away, etc. — risks undervaluing and forgetting the treasure of personal, heart-to-heart relationships. It is through relationships, through love, that we are fulfilled.

Relationships imply openness, vulnerability, presence towards others, a way of listening to, understanding, and caring for others that reveals to them their value and their gifts. When we love and respect people, revealing to them their value, they can begin to come out from behind the walls that protect them. They are no longer frightened of being hurt; they can begin to open up.

Corrymeela, a peacemaking community in Northern Ireland, brought together mothers and wives of men killed by the IRA with mothers and wives of people killed by the loyalist paramilitary. They wept together and realized the senselessness of the civil war and of vengeance. U.S. Senator George Mitchell did something similar in Northern Ireland when he helped leaders from the two sides move from a place of grievance to a place of personal encounter. He took them out to dinner and asked them not to speak about their rights or politics, their hurts or grievances, but about their families, their leisure activities. We begin to move towards peace as we move away from our own labels and the labels we have put on others, and meet heart to heart, person to person.

Trust is born and we live a true encounter.

This process is not easy. I remember a meeting I attended in Ottawa in the 1970s with people in the Canadian correctional system: inmates, ex-inmates, guards, prison directors, chaplains, psychologists. We slept in the dormitory of a former prison that had been converted into a youth hostel. Each of us was identified by just a name badge — no information about our roles, our jobs, our titles. How much simpler it would have been to "know" people by categorizing them, labelling them as belonging to one group or another, defining them by our notions of "us" and "them." It was a slow and delicate journey to start from scratch, to get to know each other based only on our individual meetings, on our mutual interest and curiosity.

Personal relationship implies tenderness and kindness. The opposite of love is hardness of the heart or insensitivity; it is indifference to others and to what they think, feel, and need. It is to avoid meeting them and to erect defence mechanisms. Fear encloses people within their systems of protection. Peace is not just absence of war and it is not just living alongside others, ignoring them, indifferent to them, or avoiding them. Peace is getting to know each other, appreciating each other, seeing each other's value, and receiving from each other. It flows from a

communion of hearts in which we discover that we
are truly brothers and sisters belonging to a common
humanity. This communion of hearts is not just sentimental; it does not mean merely sheltering amidst a
friendly group. It implies that together, as a community and as friends, we are committed to working for
peace and justice. Peace is the fruit of love, a love that
is also justice. But to grow in love requires work —
hard work. And it can bring pain because it implies
loss — loss of the certitudes, comforts, and hurts that
shelter and define us.

Risk

Those who seek encounters with those who are different do not always know where the relationship
will lead. To love is always a risk: it can mean rejection and marginalization by the secure group one
belongs to; it can mean pain in the relationship itself.
To love in this way can cause a loss of security, even a
loss of friends from one's own culture who remain
stuck behind categories and do not understand.

The Serbian Orthodox priest and the German
army captain let their deepest persons emerge from
behind all the fear and compulsion for success, security, and admiration that may have governed their
lives. They chose not to be imprisoned in their own
culture or by what others wanted of them. Some in

authority may even have seen them as traitors. They felt free to be themselves and to follow their own personal conscience, enlightened by God; free to be as compassionate as the Samaritan who saved an enemy lying wounded on the wayside;[8] free to go against established customs and categories in order to follow the urgings of love and peace engraved in our hearts.

FORGIVENESS

When German tanks rolled onto her family property in southern France in 1940, Maïti Girtanner, a young Frenchwoman, was appalled, and decided to join the resistance movement. She was eventually captured and tortured by a German doctor who specialized in crippling people by interfering with their central nervous system. She was the only one of twenty who survived, but she lived afterwards in constant, excruciating pain. In 1984, in her simple apartment near Paris, she received a phone call and immediately recognized the voice as that of the German doctor. They met and shared together. She was able to forgive him. He had become the mayor of a small town in Austria, and on his return home from his visit with Maïti, he gathered together his family and the villagers and he told them the truth about his life. Two weeks later he died of cancer.[9]

When we have been hurt deeply by a person or a

group, a wound is created in us. We are angry and want vengeance, as in the parable of the factory supervisor who yelled unjustly at the worker, causing the worker to inflict his anger and anguish upon his wife: "You have hurt me, so I will find relief in hurting you or someone else." Wounds fester and gangrene sets in. The guilt and depression in us becomes an energy that can turn into conflict.

Jewish people can remain victims of historical mistreatment and the Holocaust, and Palestinians may seek revenge for being driven from their homes and country. Hindus and Muslims in India, Christians and Muslims in Indonesia, Catholics and Protestants in Northern Ireland, blacks and whites in South Africa — the history of hurts and injustice is long. Can peace come if there is no healing of memories? Is it possible to forgive the person or the group who in some way has damaged my life, reduced my freedom, or killed my friends? "Ultimately we have just one moral duty," wrote Etty Hillesum. "To reclaim large areas of peace and to reflect it towards others. And the more peace there is in us, the more peace there will be in our troubled world."[10]

I think often of a group of Catholic monks who lived in a town about forty kilometres from Algiers and were extremely friendly with the local Muslim community. In 1996, seven of the monks were murdered as part of a political insurgence. Christian Chergé, the head of the monastery, had written a letter to be opened at his death and sent it to his mother in Paris. In it he thanks his parents, relatives, brother monks, and friends — and someone unexpected:

> In this "thank you," which is said for everything in my life, I certainly include you, friends of yesterday and today . . . and you also, friend of my final moment, who would not be aware of what you are doing. Yes, for you too, I want to say this "thank you" and "à Dieu" [to God], whom I have seen through you. May we meet again in Paradise as two blessed and good thieves, if that is what God, the Father of us both, wants. Amen! Inch'Allah![11]

To look forward, to want life, means we have to be willing to look backwards and become more conscious of all those who have hurt us, all that is broken in us and that has brought us inner deaths, hurts that we may have hidden and stifled. It means that we acknowledge the story of our origins, of our own lives, see and accept our brokenness and the times we also have hurt others. When we have accepted who we are and what we need in order to grow in compassion and peacemaking, we can move forward to give life. To forgive is a gift of God that permits us to let go of our past hurts. As John Paul II says, "There is no peace without justice and no justice without forgiveness."[12]

I don't believe that forgiveness springs up *naturally* in us. What springs from within us is often vengeance, revenge, depression, and anger. But the gift of forgiveness can be given. We can grow in the desire to live in the present moment and to embrace the future, and it is only through this grace that comes from God, this power to forgive others and ourselves, that we can begin to meet each other. I believe that one day we will discover that the hurts we have lived can become a source of life; new energies will spring from our wounds. In each one of us there is this life, this power, that can lead us forward. We must recognize the wound. It is there. But when we also recognize that we are loved by God we can live something extraordinary. We can receive the gift of forgiveness.

Freedom

In his book *The Needs of Strangers*, philosopher and historian Michael Ignatieff distinguishes between basic needs of human beings and the needs that, if respected, allow people not only to survive but to blossom and become fulfilled. Our basic needs are food, lodging, education, and medical help; our other needs are to be loved, appreciated, respected, and seen as valuable. Ignatieff argues that ensuring the basic needs of people is an act of justice that can be regulated by law, but helping a person to be fulfilled through love can never be regulated or imposed by law; you cannot oblige someone to love another because love is something that flows from our freedom. A child needs the fulfillment of basic needs but also fulfillment of the fundamental need for love. There can be no real peace if we simply remain respectful of law. Love calls forth what is deepest in each person, and if there is no real love, then there is no real peace, and justice is not respected.

The United Nations Declaration of Human Rights and Freedoms has deepened the consciousness of the importance of each and every person. But who is the person? What is the ultimate value of a human being? I mentioned earlier that human beings search unceasingly for the infinite. We are never fully satisfied by the limited. And as we have seen, there is an anguish in us that pushes us to look for more — more power, more pleasure, more money, more love, more friends, more knowledge, more experience, and, I would say, more God! Humanity is always in movement, always evolving, searching, hoping — and at the heart of each person there is this yearning for the unlimited, for the infinite.

This search reveals the sacred in each human

being. This sacredness is not disconnected from our bodies. The infinite is made flesh in our bodies, and our bodies are connected to the earth and to the universe. All things are interconnected, all life. Every species is important and precious. This thirst for the infinite can only begin to be quenched when in some way we experience the Infinite and are in relationship with it. We can break through the closed security of family, culture, and group and meet each other as precious only if we discover that, over and above every family and culture, there is a universal truth and justice that permits us to see people in their rightful place.

Crossing the barriers among us requires us to embrace our deepest fears — to risk rejection, hurt, pain, and loneliness, to move beyond the security of the past and sometimes our culture, and to live for the present and the future. To nurture peace we must search out openness, risk, forgiveness, and freedom to find not only what is sacred in others, but what is sacred within ourselves. We can become brothers and sisters in a common humanity only if we discover a God who is Father and Mother to us all, the God who is above all that is limited. The philosopher Søren Kierkegaard affirmed this too, when he said that our equality lies in the fact that we are all equally loved by God. How often we ignore this simple, sacred truth.

IV

CROSSING THE BARRIERS
WITHIN US

WE CAN BE SEDUCED by publicity, made to think that in order to be happy we must buy and use a highly advertised product. Doesn't television thrive on publicity? We can be seduced also by powerful political groups that promise more wealth and lower taxes. Those with power can use clever, psychological tricks and play upon our weaknesses and brokenness in order to attract us to their way of thinking. We can be manipulated into illusion.

Our danger is to think that happiness will come from outside of us, from the things we possess or the power of our group, and not from within us, from the inner sanctuary of our being. How quickly we human beings fall into illusion, the illusion that we are the centre of the universe — or the opposite extreme, the illusion that we are nobody. And how easily we imagine that if we are part of this or that group or gain more money, all will be well. We can all be seduced by false prophets who promise happiness. But when we submit to these illusions, very quickly we lose our true selves and end up falling into a paralysis of anger or despair. Depression can overcome us. We are ashamed that reality and illusion do not coincide, ashamed even of our existence.

Happiness is accepting and choosing life, not just submitting grudgingly to it. It comes when we *choose* to be who we are, to be ourselves, at this present moment of our lives; we choose life as it is, with all its joys, pain, and conflicts. Happiness is living and seeking the truth, together with others in community, and assuming responsibility for our lives and the lives of others. It is accepting the fact that we are not infinite, but can enter into a personal relationship with the Infinite, discovering the universal truth and justice that transcends all cultures: each person is unique and sacred. We are not just seeking to be what others want us to be or to conform to the expectations of family, friends, or local ways of being. We have chosen to be who we are, with all that is beautiful and broken in us. We do not slip away from life and live in a world of illusions, dreams, or nightmares. We become present to reality and to life so that we are free to live according to our personal conscience, our sacred sanctuary, where love resides within us and we see others as they are in the depth of their being. We are not letting the light of life within us be crushed, and we are not crushing it in others. On the contrary, all we want is for the light of others to shine.

Peace of heart is something very personal that flows from within us. It can come through a personal accomplishment, works of justice and mercy, or acts of kindness. It can come as we live in harmony with our family or community, or in quiet moments of reflection and inner acceptance. The German theologian Josef Pieper speaks of leisure as that time when we can be alone with "that silence which is a prerequisite to the apprehension of reality; only the silent hear."

> Given the pressures in the marketplace, we need to be vigilant and alert to hostile influences which demean our dignity. One of the most insidious traps is self-hate. Leisure is only possible when we are at one with ourselves. We tend to overwork as a means of self-escape, as a way of trying to justify our existence. There is only one justification for our existence: God loves us. We fear relaxing and letting go because we lack trust in love. And so we are always in control, always in haste, lest if we slow down we face ourselves. It is no dramatic over-statement to say that the basis of all joy and happiness

and creativity is humble self-acceptance. This self-
acceptance is the basis of freedom and holiness.[13]

— and, I would add, of peace of heart. Pieper goes on
to say that to acquire inner stillness, "there is
absolutely no substitute for prayer and reflection. We
must hear God's plea: 'Be still and know me.'"

Peace is not just the suppression of our desire for
things or status, but rather the fulfillment of our deepest needs. Peace is the fruit of a personal relationship
with the Eternal. We are not alone. God, gentle and
humble, is with us, watching over us and guiding us.
As we relax and trust in love we become free of the
walls and barriers that imprison us in fear, prejudice,
and guilt. We are filled with a new joy, a new life,
the very life of love. We experience a new strength: the
peace that springs from the loving, tender *presence* of
God. We no longer need to prove ourselves; we can be
ourselves with all our fragility, vulnerability, and
weaknesses. We are precious to God just as we are.

Etty Hillesum had a deep sense of the value of
each person as the "home" of God. When she was in
Westerbrook with other Jews waiting for their final
hour of deportation to Auschwitz, she wrote in her
diary that her only desire was to help people discover
the treasure of their personhood, that each of them
was called to be the "home" of God:

And I promise You [my God], yes, I promise that I shall try to find a "home" and a refuge for You in as many houses as possible. There are so many empty houses, and I shall prepare them all for You as guest of honour.[14]

She was aware of the secret: the beauty of every person is that they are called to become a home for the Infinite, to no longer be plagued by fear of the limited and of death. Her insights came in a situation of horrible adversity; out of the most terrible, ugliest realities a new and deeper vision arose, and light flowed from the darkness:

And there are those [detained Jews] who want to put their bodies in safekeeping but who are nothing more than a shelter for a thousand fears and bitter feelings. And they say "I shan't let them [the Nazis] get me into their clutches." But they forget that no one is in their clutches who is in Your arms. I am beginning to feel a little bit more peaceful, God, thanks to this conversation with You.[15]

We become peacemakers as we let ourselves be disarmed, as we become more conscious that we are — each of us — unique and, in the words of Etty Hillesum, held in the arms of God. We are not alone, and we don't have to compete. Our place in the heart of humanity and in the heart of God is assured. We are meant to live in and bring peace. To become fully human is to become conscious of who we are in the depths of our being, conscious of this thirst for the infinite, and to discover that we can find the Infinite, the Eternal, within us, within our inner sanctuary. This life with God is like a spring of living water within us that is often covered up with a lot of muck and rubble, hidden behind the barriers of fear.

We Need to Be Cleansed

These barriers or walls within us hold back all our anguish, but also what is most beautiful in us. We have to be cleansed of the need to divide the world, society, groups, and individuals into "good" and "bad," placing our own group, country, religion, class as the elite, the best. Above all, we are called to let go of our compulsions and be purified of our thirst for power, for admiration, and for righteousness. Our walls of fear, prejudice, and hate must gradually come down so that we be liberated from the enclosures that prevent us from becoming open to a new knowledge of the Infinite and of others.

But the journey to humility, peace, and justice is a long and arduous struggle, as Patriarch Athenagoras of Constantinople makes so clear in his confessional poem, "I Am Disarmed":

I have waged this war against myself for many years.
It was terrible.
But now I am disarmed.
I am no longer frightened of anything
because love banishes fear.
I am disarmed of the need to be right
and to justify myself by disqualifying others.
I am no longer on the defensive
holding onto my riches.
I just want to welcome and to share.
I don't hold onto my ideas and projects.
If someone shows me something better —
No, I shouldn't say better but good —
I accept them without any regrets.
I no longer seek to compare.
What is good, true and real is always for me the best.
That is why I have no fear.
When we are disarmed and dispossessed of self
If we open our hearts to the God-Man
who makes all things new
then He takes away past hurts
and reveals a new time
where everything is possible.[16]

This road to the emergence of self, of our deepest person, with a sense of who we are and of our mission in life, is a long one. It is the story of a lifetime and can imply many struggles. We all have to *work* at it! Jesus tells a parable about a grain of wheat, about how our psychological compulsions are called to die so that in time we can live fully and bear much fruit.[17] It takes time, the work of grace, and the help of wise people for us to become sufficiently humble and transformed, to become a home for love and for the Infinite where the living waters of love and compassion flow from the centre of our being. We all need to be cleansed so that, as Etty Hillesum says in her diary, we can be "a balm for all wounds."[18]

This cleansing is not something we can do by ourselves, by our own willpower or self-control. It is deeper than that. It is done through acceptance of certain events that may break or hurt us; it is done with the help of wise men and women; and it is accomplished through a gift of God, who leads us into greater life and to greater freedom. The road to peace and hope is paved by a well-knit and open family and by roots in a culture, a faith, and a community that give us security, form us, prepare us to go forward, awaken and strengthen our personal conscience, and help us to discover who we are. We need models, a spiritual father and mother who are wise and free and who call us to grow in freedom, wisdom, compassion, and openness to others who are different. We will live unexpected events, loss, pain, accidents, failure, joy and success, and unexpected meetings with others. We are called to live fully every one of these events according to our conscience, not letting ourselves be submerged by life or drowned by the grief of unhappy events.

I know how much I myself still need to be cleansed. When I've been faced with people who challenge me, or whose anguish and disordered behaviour awaken anguish in me, I have experienced anger and violence within. There are still barriers and fears in me that prevent me from being compassionate and open to some people. And when I feel lost, I turn to the people around me, to the prophets of peace who, unknown and unrecognized, are sowing the seeds of peace in our world. They have made the long journey to self-acceptance and purification, recognizing what is sacred and universal. I think of them as they nurture hope and love in individual hearts, finding and spreading peace in small communities around the globe, and I remember that each of us *can* change, that in the presence of isolation, anguish, terror, and violence, individuals — you and I — can unleash a torrent of loving kindness that will change the world.

V

FINDING PEACE

ONE DAY WE WELCOMED into our L'Arche home in Bangalore, India, a young lad with severe disabilities who had been living in the streets. He was hungry and covered in dirt. By the little hat he was wearing, we knew he was Muslim. Cham, one of the men with disabilities who had been living in the home for quite some time and who was from a Brahman family, offered to share his room with this newcomer. Little by little, "Abdul" — the name the community gave to him, as he was unable to communicate his real name — opened up. He learned to walk and to do many of the same things as the other residents. One day an assistant accompanied him to a local mosque. Suddenly a voice cried out, "Elias!" It was "Abdul's" cousin. The lost boy had been found.

A few days later a whole Muslim family arrived at our house. The elderly father told us, "My son is happy with you. He has made so much progress. We want him to stay with you." A friendship has grown between the L'Arche community and the family. And so sometimes it is the weakest ones, the least recognized, who can bring together people who are very different — not only in the community but also among neighbours, friends, and family — and set us on the path to peace.

In our communities in India, Christians, Muslims, and Hindus live together. We cannot say that there are no difficulties in those communities — there are all the same difficulties of living together as you might find among people of different ages, temperaments, needs, and stories who come from the same faith tradition! But we are all part of a common humanity and of a vast and beautiful universe, and each person has something to offer to us if we receive their gift, and learn to appreciate the cultures in which others have grown and developed, even if at first they appear strange. Together we gradually discover that difference, though painful, can be a treasure, not a threat. Joy and freedom come as we accept the pain of difference. In that way, communities can be a sign of peace and unity. My own experience living in L'Arche has shown me that community is the place where we can be healed and the milieu in which we can grow to that inner freedom necessary for us to become healers and peacemakers.

Community is a place of belonging where people, though very different in temperament and background, and who do not necessarily live under the same roof, discover others of like mind and spirit who love and appreciate each other and reveal to each who they are. It is a place where they grow in maturity and can find inner healing. They learn also to accept themselves and others as they are. And when they are bonded together, they learn forgiveness. Community is authentic only if all of its members are encouraged to assume and surpass their fears of loneliness, to develop greater inner freedom, to forgive, and to become more fully themselves, without hiding inside or behind the group. If obedience inside of the group is too rigid, it can stifle the growth of personal conscience and inner freedom.

If community members are open to those who are different, inside or outside the community, they become a sign and source of peace. As they come together and give each other support, they welcome people and accomplish things they could not do alone. They can confront difficulties and walk bravely through the fear and pain of life. When community or fellowship is lived fully and authentically, when members are united and prepared to work through the conflicts inherent in all groups of people, when they are seeking to grow in their mission of compassion to those in need, the community can become a sign of our collective potential, of what we can become if we all leave behind selfishness and individual needs and share and work together for greater peace and unity.

Peacemaking

Peacemaking is not just doing big things to solve big conflicts, in the way of Nelson Mandela, Mahatma Gandhi, or George Mitchell. We are not all called to work for peace on the international level, but we are all called to become men and women of peace wherever we may be — in our family, at work, in our parish, in our neighbourhood — open and welcoming to others inside and outside of our community, our culture, and our faith group. To be a peacemaker means not to judge or condemn or speak badly of people, not to rejoice in any form of ill that may strike them. Peacemaking is holding people gently in prayer, wishing them to be well and free. Peacemaking is welcoming people who are weak and in need, maybe just with a smile, giving them support, offering them kindness and tenderness, and opening our hearts to them. It is welcoming those with whom we may have difficulty or whom we may not especially like, those who are culturally, psychologically, or intellectually different from us. It is to approach people not from a pedestal, a position of power and certitude, in order to solve problems, but from a place of listening, understanding, humility, and love. When we relinquish power, we become more open to the compassion of God.

We work for peace every time we exercise authority with wisdom and authentic love. This love is not sentimental; it reveals to people who they are, enabling them to make choices and to follow their consciences. It is listening to people and appreciating them just as they are. We need to become humble servant-leaders in order to help others grow in knowledge, wisdom, freedom, and responsibility, so that they may become, in the depth of their beings, more human. When we love people, we liberate them. To be good leaders we also have to be prepared to let go of authority and let others continue the work of leadership when the time comes.

Prophets of peace are those who in their person and attitudes do not awaken fear, but open people's hearts to understanding and compassion. They are those who are weak and who are crying out for relationship. In some mysterious way they are breaking down the barriers of fear in our hearts. What happens when we start becoming attentive to the weak? We begin to accept our own weaknesses. We discover that there are a lot of things we can't do, that we need others! It is when we discover our vulnerability and fragility that we begin to move out from behind the barriers we put around our hearts to protect our-selves. We begin to build community. We can then cry out, "I need help — from my friends, my family, my faith, my God, my community, and others. I need help to love and forgive people."

We become prophets of peace when we discover our weakness. Here we are touching a mystery. Peace doesn't come from superiority and might. It comes from this power of life that flows from the deepest, most vulnerable part of our being, a power of gentle and strong life that is in you and in me.

Not long ago I spent a weekend in a Christian parish near Paris. On the Sunday morning I met with children from three to seven years old, then with children from eight to twelve, and then with adolescents from thirteen to seventeen. Later I met with the adults. I was amazed that it was the first group of children — those between three and seven years old — who asked me the most questions! They seemed to be free of group pressure, of what the others might think of them. The innocence, purity, and simplicity of those children, who had found real security in their families, were disarming. Young children have a way of calling forth the simplicity of our own hearts, our childlikeness, which is hidden behind our self-consciousness and the fear of what others might think. They awaken our hearts. They do not provoke fear. They break down our defence systems and our prejudices. Children have a way of accepting others as they are, without prejudice, without fear, as long as they are in a place of security. They trust quickly if they feel trusted. Whether they be Christian, Muslim, Buddhist, Hindu, or Jewish, children have a mysterious power to break down the inner barriers that prevent us from being open to people of other cultures; they inspire us to call forth the child within ourselves.

This same power is found in many men and women with intellectual disabilities. Though less capable in some ways, people with disabilities are often endowed with simple, loving, and trusting hearts. They show a path to love rather than to power. In our L'Arche and Faith and Light communities they have an incredible way of welcoming people. So often they are filled with a joie de vivre that attracts and opens hearts and brings joy. They are often less complicated than those who are caught up in the need for success, power, and admiration. Their cry is not so much for admiration as for simple, faithful relationship.

I recently received a letter from Philip Kearney of
L'Arche, who was in Jerusalem for a sabbatical,
telling me about a group of eight men who have
severe intellectual and physical disabilities. Two are
Palestinian Muslims, three are Palestinian Christians,
and three are Israeli Jews. They are quite happy to be
together and to meet and talk with others; they radi-
ate a peace that is not found in those in the larger
community.

> Once a week I go for a walk with this strange and
> wonderful group in the streets and parks. . . . It's quite
> an experience. Palestinians who have known them for
> many years come up and greet them by putting their
> hands on their heads in a sort of gesture of welcome
> and blessing. Then a little further on Israelis come
> up and greet the group, recognizing their own. The joy
> that these meetings give to those who approach is
> quite visible. Up until today this is the only group that
> I have met with representatives of the three great reli-
> gions of this land not only living together day by day,
> but also walking hand in hand in the streets of
> Jerusalem together!

They are prophets of peace, showing the way to
peace. Their cry for love can bring together men and
women of different faith traditions and cultural back-

grounds. They break down prejudice and call forth what is deepest in us.

A few years ago a young man with disabilities participated in the Special Olympics. He wanted so much to win the gold medal in the 100-metre race. The race began, and he made a good start, but moments later the young man in the next lane slipped and fell. The young man who had been so anxious to win immediately stopped, gave his hand to the fallen man, and pulled him up. Both continued to run, and both came in last! Our world would be a better place if we could all listen to this young man and discover that compassion and fellowship are more important than strength or winning or power.

How can we work for peace when we are faced with authority that does not listen, that cannot accept that it is not always right, and that refuses any form of criticism or dialogue? Do we leave, slamming the door? Do we seek to create a revolution? Do we let the desire for vengeance grow? Or do we fall into a form of depression and submission because there is nothing else to do? How can we be true when faced with insolent oppression and might? How can we work for justice in impossible situations?

Men and women such as Francis of Assisi, Mahatma Gandhi, Martin Luther King Jr., Dorothy Day, Aung San Suu Kyi, Corazón Aquino, Jean and

Hildegard Goss-Mayr, and so many others, hidden
and unknown, have shown a way. They are prophets
of peace. They have lived and proclaimed a path of
non-violence. They have been able to do this because
they received support and lived with a community of
men and women of like minds and hearts. "When I
despair," said Mahatma Gandhi, "I remember that
throughout history the way of truth and love has
always won. There have been tyrants and murderers
and for a time they can seem invincible. But in the
end they always fall. Think of it always . . . whenever
you are in doubt that that is God's way — the way the
world is meant to be. Think of that and then try to do
His way."

These men and women didn't attack insolent
might face on, which often only reinforces the barriers, but worked to help the powerful to step down, to
change and evolve. At the same time, they sought
to give those who were suffering injustice the freedom to work for peace, to love the truth, to not be
governed by fear and hate, to love people, and to
build community — to be themselves.

One of the great prophets of non-violence was a
devout Muslim, Ghaffar Khan, a Pashtun from the
north of India, now Pakistan. Independently of
Mahatma Gandhi, and later in collaboration with
him, he sought, through the refusal of all forms of

violence, to liberate his people from the oppressive and often cruel military rule of the British, promotion of the status of women in his country, social justice so that all in his country might have education and the necessities of life, and active collaboration with people of other religions.[19]

In our time, John Paul II, while growing older and ever more frail, continues to be a prophet of peace, travelling from country to country, proclaiming peace, asking forgiveness, bringing people of different religious faiths together, and defending the rights of each and every person, especially the poor, the weak, and minorities. I was in Haiti in 1983 when the pope celebrated mass at the Port-au-Prince airport. On his left were representatives of the Haitian dictatorship and the military; on his right, the diplomatic corps; and in front, spread over a large area, the Haitian people. He spoke of the importance of washing the feet of the poor and the weak. The crowd cheered and went wild with joy. I could not see the expressions on the faces of the government people or the military, but I can imagine they were upset. It was as if the pope were the judge, the government and military leaders in the judgement box, and the people the jury.

To become peacemakers today is to learn to live simply, with or close to people who are different or in need. For how can there be peace if people who are

in terrible need are living near people who are living in great luxury, with no contact? Living together
with people who have been devalued helps them
and us to discover their, and our, human value and
dignity.

Many people today are living in this way. This is
what we too want in our communities of L'Arche and
Faith and Light. I think also of a small group of Christian sisters in Niger who have been sharing their lives
for over twenty years with the Tuaregs, a nomadic
Muslim people who live under tents and tend herds
of goats. The sisters have their own tent and herd of
goats. They are not seeking to change the Tuaregs but
simply to be with them, to be their friends, to reveal to
them their beauty and importance. In the eyes of our
efficient world, of the competitive global marketplace,
living together in this way may seem foolish, but it is
the foolishness of the gospel message, the foolishness
of love, which is perhaps what our world needs most.

How important it is to listen to one another's stories. I think of Karin, a woman I've known for many
years through L'Arche, who lives in Wilcannia, Aus-
tralia, a little town made up largely of aboriginal
people, where about eighty percent of the inhabitants
are out of work. She does not teach or do anything
particular, but she shares their stories, their difficulties, and their daily life and has become a friend to
many, revealing the love of God just by her presence.

And I think of Ansaff, a young Muslim woman from Hebron who was an assistant in our L'Arche community in Bethany, near Jerusalem. It was beautiful to see her relationship with people who have disabilities and a privilege to listen to her story and the stories of her family and of her growth in faith and humanism.

The journey of peacemaking is not easy. It may be easy to be a *lover of* peace, but it is more difficult to be a *worker for* peace, a maker of peace, day in and day out. When difficulties and conflict arise, we can easily be discouraged. Sometimes our efforts appear so futile. We so often touch the violence within our own selves. We can fall into doubt and even confusion. To struggle for peace is to be passionate for development, so that each and every person may fulfill not only their basic needs but also the needs that allow them to blossom and become fully human. I believe it is this prophetic, silent service to those of other cultures and religions, or to those who are broken and in pain, that is needed now in our world. People like Karin, and Philip Kearney, and Christian Chergé, and the music teacher in Palestine, are present in many disadvantaged areas of our world. They are with refugees in camps, with people who have AIDS, serving and living with the weak and the broken, revealing to them that they are precious. I am touched to see the many young people today who leave their homes and go to live with and serve disadvantaged people. After a

year or more, they return transformed. Their shared
life with people of another culture breaks down their
prejudices and calls them to discover the beauty and
value of different cultures and of our common
humanity. The waters of understanding and compassion for individuals rise up within them. They are
starting on the road to peacemaking and wisdom.

Martin Luther King Jr., the great modern-era
prophet of peace and reconciliation, pronounced in
his Nobel Prize speech words that these young people are *living* and showing are as true for today and
tomorrow as they were for the day on which he spoke
them: "I believe that unarmed truth and uncondi-
tional love will have the final word in reality. This is
why right temporarily defeated is stronger than evil
triumphant. . . . I believe that what self-centered men
have torn down, men other-centered can build up."[20]

To be a peacemaker is to be a pilgrim sailing to a
new and unknown holy land. It is to be an explorer
sailing away from the broken, the divided, the known
world, through uncharted and sometimes stormy
seas, to discover new seeds of life, of unity, ready to
grow and flower. Pilgrim sailors can sometimes feel
alone as they sail the rough seas towards peace. But
they are never alone, because they are seeking the
home of God. God is with them, calling them to continue on their journey. Their hope is waiting for them.

CONCLUSION

SOME TIME AGO, when Haiti was in turmoil, I was asked to talk to a large group of Haitian young people. The theme was "What Is My Hope?" I told them, "My hope is in each one of you. My hope is in your hearts." I went on to explain: "I have seen many men and women who were filled with anger and anguish when they arrived in L'Arche, from painful institutions or from the streets, rise up as new people filled with kindness and love. Healing and inner peace took time. I have seen young people transformed by their shared life with people with disabilities and the discovery of their own capacity to give life and hope to others. Yes, I believe in the capacity of each one of us to change."

Our world is a place of violence and fear, a place

where many hide behind walls of individualism, comfort, and security, frightened of looking at reality, unable to discern who they really are. Since September 11, 2001, many are also hiding behind prejudices and fear, stigmatizing those of other cultures. And perhaps in our times the darkness will grow darker, more towers and certitudes will crumble, and stock exchanges will wobble again before more of us truly begin to search for new ways of living, new ways of peace.

The world will not, of course, change overnight. But the gravity of our times, the fear of war, terrorism, and all forms of violence are inciting many men and women to search for a new way of life. Many have seen through the shallowness of material prosperity and are discovering that they can be an active part of peacemaking.

If you and I seek today to live peace, to be peacemakers, to help create communities of peace, it is not just to seek success. If we find peace, live and work for peace, even if we see no tangible results, we can become fully human beings, walking together on the road of kindness, compassion, and peace. New hope is born.

Lord, make me an instrument of Your peace;
where there is hatred, let me sow love;
where there is injury, pardon;
where there is doubt, faith;
where there is despair, hope;
where there is darkness, light;
and where there is sadness, joy.

O Divine Master, grant that I may not so much seek to be consoled as to console, to be understood as to understand, to be loved as to love;

for it is in giving that we receive; it is in pardoning that we are pardoned; it is in dying that we are born to eternal life.

— prayer of Francis of Assisi, 1226

Notes

Quotations from the Bible in this work are from the Revised Standard Edition or are Jean Vanier's direct translations from the Greek. Quotations from Etty Hillesum in this work are from the English language edition or are Jean Vanier's direct translations from the original Dutch.

1. Etty Hillesum, *An Interrupted Life: The Diaries, 1941– 1943, and Letters from Westerbrook* (New York: Henry Holt, 1996), 208.
2. Nassar Ibrahim and Majed Nassar, *Cry Freedom: The Palestinian Intifada* (Beit Sahour, 2002).
3. See Sigmund Freud, "Mourning and Melancholia," in Vol. 11, *On Metapsychology*, of the Penguin Freud Library (London: Penguin, 1984), 245–68.
4. Etty Hillesum, 134.
5. Mahatma Gandhi, *In Search of the Supreme*, Vol. 1 (Kathmandu: Nava Jivan Press, 1951), 44.
6. Isaiah 11:6. The prophet Hosea has a similar vision of peace: "And I will make for you a covenant on that day with the beasts of the fields, the birds of the air, and the creeping things of the ground; and I will abolish the bow, the sword, and the war from the land; and I will make you lie down in safety." (Hos 2:18).
7. See Wladyslaw Szpilman, *The Pianist* (London: Phoenix, 1995).

8. "Jesus said: A man was going down from Jerusalem to Jericho, when he fell into the hands of robbers. They stripped him of his clothes, beat him and went away leaving him half-dead. A priest happened to be going down the same road, and when he saw the man, he passed by on the other side. So, too, a Levite, when he came to the place and saw him, passed by on the other side. But a Samaritan, as he travelled, came where the man was; and when he saw him, he took pity on him. He went to him and bandaged his wounds, pouring on oil and wine. Then he put the man on his own donkey, brought him to an inn and took care of him. The next day he took out two silver coins and gave them to the innkeeper, 'Look after him,' he said, 'and when I return I will reimburse you for any extra expense you may have.'" (Luke 10:30–35).

9. See Michel Farin's film Résistance et pardon (cfrt France 2, 1998), the text of the film published by Vie Chrétienne in Paris, or www.lejourduseigneur.com.

10. Etty Hillesum, 218.

11. Christian de Chergé, "Testament," *The Tablet* (June 8, 1996).

12. This comes from His Holiness Pope John Paul II's address from Vatican City on the World Day of Peace, January 1, 2002.

13. Josef Pieper, *Leisure: The Basis of Culture* (Chicago: St. Augustine Press, 1998).

14. Etty Hillesum, 205.

15. Etty Hillesum, 178.
16. This is Jean Vanier's translation from the French of "I Am Disarmed," a poem by Athenagoras, the ecumenical patriarch of Constantinople from 1948 to 1972, which appeared in *Revue Tychique*, No. 136, November 1998.
17. Jesus gained many followers after he raised Lazarus from the dead, but he also gained many enemies. It was a time of growing hostility among people, but Jesus called for peace and brotherhood: "Truly, truly, I say to you, unless a grain of wheat falls into the earth and dies, it remains alone; but if it dies, it bears much fruit." (John 12:24).
18. Etty Hillesum, 231.
19. Robert C. Johnson, "Radical Islam and Non-Violence," *Journal of Peace Research* (University of Notre Dame) 1997, 1: 53–77. Ghaffar Khan's followers signed a ten-point pledge which read in part, "I promise to serve humanity in the name of God. . . . I promise to refrain from violence. . . . I promise to forgive those who oppress me or treat me with cruelty. . . . I promise to live a simple life."
20. See "Martin Luther King's Nobel Prize Acceptance Speech," www.nobelprizes.com.